Tattered by Magnets
12 lines 12 poems 12 twelves

Tim Allen

NEWTON-LE-WILLOWS

Published in the United Kingdom in 2014
by The Knives Forks And Spoons Press,
122 Birley Street,
Newton-le-Willows,
Merseyside,
WA12 9UN.

ISBN 978-1-909443-29-7

Acknowledgments:

Earlier versions of 2:1, 2:2, 2:3 & 2:4 appeared on Stride

Jacket illustration: Terry Hackman

Some influences need time to mature.

Ces formes déguisées que s'accablent dans l'ombre (Pierre Reverdy)

And don't beg for silver paper when I'm trying to sell you cheese (Keith Reid)

Also by Tim Allen:

Don't Start Me Talking - Ed. with Andrew Duncan (Salt, 2006).
Sea Ex/Change (itinerant, 2007).
Settings (Shearsman, 2009).
incidental harvest (Oystercatcher, 2011).
An Anabranch with Slug (Knives Forks and Spoons, 2011).
The Voice Thrower (Shearsman, 2012).
The Carousing Duck (zimZalla 2013)
© (Department 2014)

Table of Contents

1: the Months the Magnets

1:1

bait orange stone experience or

more difference leased hatch

hum of pink direct kink stray from experience

bait orange stone drag into box

bolt range stone experience or more different than yours

bait orange tone experience or make a difference more like mine

tame changed stone experience or stay hatched

hum of link direct from experience or tape orange stone

mute hum of pink ink or baste pink stone

pink strays or stays around thatched rag

into box straight into your box mauve twirl

a sequence of black and orange feathers coincidence room

1:2

table window yard   garden wrist rest

pen paper   window path   sky table rest

hand blush   shrub book   loose pebble finger cup

balloon full of cerebral sand doubt   a physical cert

arm ex   tension   heart roasting in inaudible joy cups

hart roasting   stoned   outbuilding   parky

prison visitor locked in the   conservatory   waiting

sky in detention   eyes attend   artificial evening sun

bosom of shared sand   liquid cap   the verbal eye

head and wrist turned   imploded stone peaked

sky swallow sea of biscuit cold tea   the official morning sun

elbow mountain   table lake   internal   glazing

1:3

arc   smile limb   mile   lime   acre   transit

crack   smile eliminate   aid   and   abet

lug   pulse lime   acre   dance of the pale magnets

glue   simile   doll lido   mild&   groggy

a glut of mimics a looby loo of bubbles plus a shoal of dedications

ludic   lucid   sandwiched&   layered

players jump   player's bimbo   players' prayer bimbo

beano   the Beano   player's beano   lubrication

free frozen snow   air hostess's complimentary Beano

rising air hostess   high cost of temple upkeep

a lair of players a pilot of gulfs a sherbet lemon of fuggy pressure

arcing bile   unseasonal   layer cake   limbo

1:4

invisible fade in concoction   imagines moonlight in tubes

silent fade in voice to capture hearts   rows drowning boat

shorthand solution   dissolves   witty love

cross at there being daft connection   try cricket faded green

delightful invention   roseprint   tension

current of roseprint   sharp bulge

mooncrack   blind spot pew

faded correction   also   slow s

fad   ring the best little night   behind you

ring-fenced voice half staffs for you   lent

shorthand for a dissolving parrot   in undetectable white

self-correcting fox cubs curl straight around the Mandelbrot

1:5

bubbles   static   bridging

facets   predictive   loners

white   Inuit   questing   gestures

nasal   reflected   purposes

sarcastic bubble   small panther   in the mall

intensive ribbing   rat-a-tat-tat   silhouette

musical bubble   listen please   such clean sound

pulled thought   identical   fin   tort

lubricated hatch   vaporous reverb   spotlight

face shipped in   frag   ment (gesticule – unit of gesticulation)

unusual bubble activity   all systems   crouching   grotto

bubbling grotto   toes re   fracted   vestibule

1:6

addict	didact	table made	dark valleys
addicted	didacticed	chair made	upturned tables
deictic	don't know what that means		do now and now
appropriate	always meant what that knew		don't now

don't go there   ritually   addicted   listener's sleep

valley made of millions of small valleys made terra-cotta knives

able to dame   dickhead   prize fight   how's know now

addicted already to upturned valleys made of what we've heard

went down the hills   to the sky that spoke its language

up the blues   up the reds   up the greens

up the already known   down unknown streets of darkness

hair   on   end   dictator can't do a thing with it

1:7

rustle of chance　　　rustle　　　　enhance rustle　　　　of chance

repetition of rustle　　　　　　repetition of chance rustle　of chance

rustle of repetition　　　　　reputation of chance polystyrene cactus

rotation　　　all those little boats　　　　their rough calculations

music isn't necessarily bilingual　　orchestra cottage horror

anthropologist dangles on the radio　　　　bloody reverse　　　　chase

novelist dangles off/on the radio　　　　rustle of orchestra

litres of rushing back through gushing to repeat gush in frantic reverse

magnets　　　a desert of exhausted magnets　　　rustle leveled up

magnetic rust　　　a dead sea of uphill doors　　　　hotel tail

puddles of metal　　signals of residual fatigue　　　　deity

dreaming dream equation the body is empty　　　forgone repetition

1:8

singing lies   i've heard that song before   curtsey

singing lies   i've heard those lies before   smash

smashing guess   seasick ankle bracelet awake   faint

feign encounter   i've thought that smash before   feint

gravedigger calculates disintegrating spiral of panic's limits

call it a business no call it a company   a flat indifferent curtsey

the bridge smashes into the wrist   conversing scents

a different faint stream of fluctuations   adjectival allegiance

sung lines introduce rotary gentry   invitation

invite paranoia   saint regretful   wave back

near   nearer now   here now   sprout

sprouted out of the Japanese pushchair   rubber   crown

1:9

hold ing imagin ary revolut ion b ack   love rolls

l ove ro lls in   takes joken food   prou dly

so holding imaginary revolution back   ambush

love rolls in proudly   drinks deference to   tramp wind

tr amp surpr ise pa rty   articulate car

amp lifier pa uses for reflect ion   gives joke   back

so tramp's surprise party   floats on sweat

boo   boo complicate   waiting for nothing is a   trade

shiver   whoever   identical   drama

defer   warm shambles   proudly agree

held   held back   identical   drama

imagin ary c alm imagin ary eff ect   so   proudly   copied

1:10

black   black summer   black summer idea

shoot the ceremony   in the dark

a cardiac suspense   redefined   in the corner in the back

black   black torch   an idea poking out of a sack

suspended corner   old boiler colony

the radiator has its critics   drugged   pot boiler

dragged into the black light   of an ambient   swivel

suspended sugar rat   on   ceremony

wing hip   on the way to the audition   whistling blandly

wing hip   lacking blocked feeling   tree surgeon

bracken lily mummer   chimney breast man

shot in the back   by   chicken blackleg torch operation idea

1:11

elaborate diversion airship worship park   between

clearings   caravan on all fours in a clearing house

article on suicide article on life after death   discredited

clearing   imagination in the coffin like a cup final

affection   hair   sunny and chair   thank you

thank you   chair   insulated argument   thanks

basic version   chair   vistas of instrumentation

stats on instruments   aesthetic satisfaction   rank

elaborate rose   elaborate pink orange skank electric rose

don't use adjectives to describe abstract nouns you   dildo

articles off   dial   wisecrack   air

intervening spark dismissed by designer for being too chair

1:12

water trusts glass   glass trusts water   wordlight snap

wordwater wordtrust   warp   elastic   content

Arp word   part harp world   engine sleeping cap

water rusts lass   glass trusts   suspect

suspicion thins   in   sucked in   sense

windmill trusts   these snow cherries and rational flowers

watermill's waterwheel rusts bright brown   engine sense

windmill's sails sail childlike like a national costume content string

water still trusts glass   glass no longer trusts water

blue warp of bottled water   bleeds warp of wordlight's snap

night sense   house sense   star maker

water no longer   subversive people and their childish agonies

2: the Days the Dead

2:1

neat device   adverb outsmart   silencer

capitalism exists only behind the eyes   motto

the radiation have   smart reactions   ditto

novice   digging breeze   creaking   scenery

function   lubrication   luminously   ditto

fact   reverb   silicon landscape   camouflaged

teen wave   painted   phonemes   ditto

novice   duplicates   hormonal suburbs   blotto

dark device behind the eyes   the eyes have inner strength

before boarding arc hind says yes to blackberry   core

duplicator fails to understand duplicated pamphlet   ditto

feed your engineers adverbs and the adverbs will report any error

2:2

put the hot flask in the cooler bag   relocated ode

prop shaft   arm wrestles   rope   steer around a petal trap

a career in the theatre   lukewarm nest   local rope

fan the old flare   relocated list   local interest

the   the   the   passive   founder   of a department

natal   department   river reeds   basket

glazed water wheel   lukewarm zest   in the department

naf   naïf   what part were you?   the exiting cathedral?

taking a shifty   having a proper look   road sign wit

slake a   snap shot   take a   diagonal stab

jigsaw shard silver in the bracken flask   shooken

flatbed Latin   tucked in unfinished   shift

2:3

is that you   reversing   quick slow quick quick slow?

so low to the crush   elsewhere injustice is international

is the kerb an enlarged friend?   light sticks to simple gestures

visitor   downstairs   minimal   gestures

exhausted spring   metallic blue   bitter   friend

translating   animal gestures   through gritted teef

recoiled   to base   threshold   graft

rehearsing your craft   singing verses around the raft

the quiet mind is as buoyant as a plucky little craft escaping trees

the enemy is quick to slow down to blow those swarming trees

shutter   random   nervous   system

sawing a window in half   directing the bed   from war

2:4

faculties	station	frock	tango	flat tire
difficulties	ration	trigger	retirement	flat tier
crippling	cuss	fan	switch	verdict
correction	to		creation	flat sunset

cult   fist of tortoise   companion of eye

in that new photograph of us as kids we're already   retiring

reluctant eye   long arthritic twist of sigh   abrasive

amongst the clutter in the room   circuit   satirical glory

moody yellow cameo   hippo   bars

four bars of our song   three bars   two bars   one

bear rears behind bars   three bears   two rabbis   none

thermals   frock volume   tango   rabies   test

2:5

stacked black layer upon layer between white

tacked back against the back drop of endless night

there upon their sheets drops of ticks

to make a survey of time you must swim against language's undertow

fostered for outmode survey with attitude ~~s~~potted

longitude and late for class again on long teen legs

scolded outmoded steroid told time and time

again helmets and spores paddle steamers and nim

ble satellites operated ~~on~~ by trinkets then

fatally published taken aback then

questioned oh any textbook will do to teach mer

maid how to waltz with gambler snob or whoever

2:6

mirror   spawn   mirror spawn   strewn

no temperature in the mirror   nothing hot nothing cold

not thing   but   looking cool   in the wall tool

in   nowhere   however deep   not out of sight

pawn   instrument   instrument cools   up

pawned   little machine hunkers down   in canoe   ribs

the little machine can yawn   it can do nothing else

the poor people of Norwich   crocodile on turntable

room   shallow   room shallow   hallowed

walls on the tool   Liverpool on the Meuse   mallet

looting going on in the mirror   looking allowed into wallet

play   where   i   can   see   you

2:7

quicklime corner   nigh   in cider   in the garden of

in an obscure corner of the reasoning mind   big hairy party

in a head of snow   nine perfectly made dogs   blotchy

zoom in   blotches   burning in   the burning chair

compost   in the garden of   rude penalty   art head

in an art of   sentimental   melt   wrap

it's only a metaphorical   trap   guttersnipe   blotch

zoom in   mosey around   intrude   red cider

part in   all aboard the   in the garden of   part out

slime supply   rhyme supplier   green honey   botch

tree of   forgotten   never for   given

quicksilver   mental   mentally applied nymph apple

2:8

insects alter Patrick   and   ambitious grains of sand

snakes alter insects   hand it to them   anthemic

cane   Sister   Patrick   a trick of the pain

the body as an abstraction   the body as dis   traction

sect   nonsense   and   ambitious rain on sand

stake   claimant   ants climb up the greasy gossamer brace

take pleasure in this lesson   Cyclops washing his clops

dry dusty heat nonsense   and   shoddy invest   igations

the mind moves without ceremony towards its own funeral

snakes after the road   via an   aqueduct

quip   equip   equipped with quips   looped

around music   music tied up kiss 'um trails   pooling

2:9

behind the beard he is   brooding   go on   ask him

behind the beard he is   bleeding   work's stopped

not a motel a mobile hotel   Paris is an   emotion

behind the Paris he is   dreading   going on   ask him

fortune teller gets up goes down to the cellar and winds up solitude

the   windows   are   in   visible

behind the window s/he is   secretly   begging

begging to have chakras   brutally   please let there be chakras

walking without passing   anything   some call it   praying

pray under pressure   appear   puffed   up

i heard   i heard a little bird   behind   snoring

barometer in the velvet saddlebag wants to inscribe my lollypop

2:10

brought up thought   bee   ebbing image

overwrought rainbow   overexposed slide   damaged moth

webbing   around   bone   belonging   to

hungover rock climbers shouldn't attempt   the overhang

that's not very good you've written better lines when hungover

vomited up thoughts   teach you   how to change the

past   gulls   overstatement   sails

yacht   made with   slugs and   sails

rain   exile   more rain   more exile

rain   slugs   more rain   more slugs

and   nails

units of bee   images of damaged children's playground

2:11

fed the turtle some news about itself   pine forest

horizontal abyss   literary economy   shelter

the turtle looks fed up   but it is not such distorted data

placid   damp   free to move with difficulty

glare   into the trees   wooden shield still growing

liability   vertical bars   horizontal freefall

miners reach a lake of older pines   such glaring distort

turtle looks up   the meaning   of fed up

moist and shy   regressed   via   duct

dizzily shy   vertigo   oliph   ant

helter-skelter   abhorrent   sentiment

remembering to remove the space to another part of the world

2:12

malicious variation   jealous region   primary off colour

variable malice   religious jealousy   prim cement

famous nerves   delicious fury   rhyming mariner

vous Flamel   previous number tu   citrus

obnoxious grace   prosperous suspicion   rind

graceful exercise   generous caution takes baking exam

ridiculous tremor left out all night   victory's   angst

various curiosities   numerous jealousies   all fastidious

the angle of the lapels was all wrong for a fatty headache tune

apart from the trade in sounds   communication was shapeless

serial virginity   mariner stop your   golden roaming

danger split stranger into   three image speed   curios

3: the Knights the Numbers

3:1

dripping off the albatross   bride passes over

whatever is ripping off the albatross it   shuns   distance

semaphore error   the bird passes over its watch

decaying customs   seal's magnetic stubble completes task

the drips above are too small to see   sad wanderer

volume of concentrated nothing   knowledge is not information

etc   etc   etc   etc

the spirit   had a birthmark   seal shaves it off

we're off   a third off etc   refuse this pattern too

Tom refuses to turn the page   egg white egg white

intellectual chaos drips up pattern   big flat vulgar bird of

top heavy drip   seal of   unique task died of its tips

3:2

bedrock glides bedrock guides

she wore a seismic shift roots torn sides

milking stool lifts guides long knives

lies infinities tournament fins in tormented bedrock

more infinities more lies irregular fines

shaft heft stained haze beam press

armchair fens sediment high in the fly zone

Victorian tiles torn from auction

built down from the top of the atmo sphere

trench has a skin arty sculpted benches that nobody can sit ~~on~~ in

pilfered shopping trolley snivels on way to school in looted bedrock

another avalanche on one leg Miss Behaved

3:3

there should have been an explosion   wait longer

dazzle comes in teams   in   decent bushes under trees

sandwiched   between   thumb of plankton and

bushes leave no room under the trees   waiting spaniel

return to the sandwich   bite   the marsh   out of Poland

pure   cane naked star shoot   marching in anger

the capital city shakes with fear   tangled in the golden briars

thrown to the ground   star chute   *bring on the wall*

there should have been an echo   wait here

saunter back   sandwiched under   tidal shale

dazzle comes in teams   lazy tousle   numb bunny girl

foaming shrubbery   sandwiched arousal   run!

3:4

grown   tree   groans   right hand   performs

river always running away with the love   lefthander reforms

scream   purpose   does a void improvise or follow a plan?

own this cabaret bottle   own this waxen face in the shadows

the next now   intrudes   no hard shoulder for 400m

dialogue   one-way street   the flying wind   formality

retro   gradual   cult scream   morph

juggler drops purpose   in a gown of light   in a gown of ash

trespass   your own   past   sheathe   the blur

tiptoe   bloated   pass   shrunken   creature

recreate   the battle   in a u-boat   in a bottle

in a bottle   in a battle   in a u-boat   put out to   pasture

3:5

Eros　　　　cattle　　　　nemesis　　　nettles　　　　creased

tittle tattled　　　　greased toss pot　　potent　　　mimesis

sorrow wow　stutter show　　　　fancy hat alternative to a hat

to wear where　　　tit-for-tat　　fancy　oracle　　　　rut

war　　peace　　　　alternate　　monograph　　　　fancy that

war　　alternative　　　　wet dream mile　　a bit of racy peace

other alternative　　to war　　　a piece of corduroy　pudding

soaring　　　to get a bit off　　　other alternatives　to peace

fancy that　　tut　　tut tut　　　afterlife lasted for a few minutes

tall　　story　　　lately　　　the show goes　　on

showboat　　greased　　painted　　　grease　　painted

a favourite Venus　　a friendly venue　　a very　　very ferry

3:6

what to do with   mouth   what to do with   breath

what to do with   stuff   what to do with   him

what to do with   sheepish bruise   heaps

sunglasses storm out of chemists   ?   lost instructions

launch without bang   lunch   lightening threatens

thunder's already threatened   the burst knot kestrel

what do do   kettle tries to explain evaporation

who's there?   aliens   land   knocking on silence

i.o.u. knocks on   shellfish   taking in a   show

what show?   do they throw their hats in the air as if they were ?s ?

keep your elbows   in the dress   what is it with you?

stuffed sheep   mid-day endures   sheep wander   off

3:7

only millions   the only same   the only mean one cleans

lonely millions   a pair   kidnapped vocabulary

only television   only capital   buried vocal

only expected   lonely cliché   shocking socks

underlined hood   4 hostages to a tune   new cliché

likelihood on trial   one average judge misjudges verge

squinting lump   splash out   added fixture

punctured princess   only a mountain ridge   on fire

plus   future departure   lounge

supple number   cleans a   hole   in nature

minus   millions   fond structure   tour

only   feature   the low millions

3:8

roadworks   droll lords   withheld universe

fringe   extermination   far from finished   advent

road works   sleepy and intimate   sand pie

fringe   annihilation   imaginary friends on a raft

shin morphs into a long long   thing   without a past

sledge   all a blur   giant ruby in bonsai rubble range

higher up on the edge of the hole far behind   ad   vantage

drawer ant   bottom drawer tenant   rum standards

bigwig   x   marks the   deemed a need

the defeated workers regroup   their children decipher signatures

diverted   immortal   a ship sailing for ever into dock

or unlike   a fringe of springs   spooling wire   catching

3:9

here comes the disorder   showbizzed   raised beach

the sea sharpens the headland   notice me

here comes the cold Sahara   popular impaction day

this programme about turtles is going on for an inordinate length of

the elephant needs to be reminded   to bring the cutlery

tricolor   what's human for bread?   is it smoke signal?

here   where affect   becomes   effect

there   where affection   becomes   effecting

here comes the horizon   variety act   raised stage

the actress sharpens her tongue   becomes   teeth

a new tricolor   pink   white   mint

scout led the hunting party singing   *mountain deep river high*

3:10

my vocabulary is not large   relativity is lexically limitless

at large   hugs and   touches   relatively   simple

haphazard   zzzzzzzz   lizard   zzzzzzzzz   zimplex

happens that   it happens that   it happens   zzzzzzzz

the moon is shaped   the road is drilled   what sounds

the dog is shaped   an unbroken stream of small irrelevancies

an unbroken shape   of dog   dogs' true   symbols

zszszszszszszszszs   a yard long kiss   down the long yard back

this moonlight is not large   in the next garden it izzzzzzz

pompom   gorse   gilt clippers   owl gets swan

mop up   soak blaze Ltd.   my ton up is not fast

upon hazard's word   beautiful evening brings out sea frontz

3:11

the clouds were put in a zoo next to the zebras behind barcodes

zebras ate the clouds as clouds emerged from the zebras' arses

the clouds were unchanged   which is pretty strange

pretty clouds   a present for the daughters of the whip

the windowsill behind the covered wagon   sonic Dante

adjusted   pill languor   journalist chews lip

adjusted   and seen to be   done   journalist smells gas

zoo was put in an ice bucket with the reporter's unchanged nappy

which is rather weird a bit like something else that's   weird

zebra   strange familiar zebra   dynastic chart

missed the point   of the swings and roundabouts

voices   blown   symbiosis ate the incoming clown vomit

3:12

hearing them talk   that human span   not in the   first place

they talk about   they talk as if   since coming out of nature

dream code   soda ghosted   first fiction

tacky spirit   heartbreaking Buddhist nun   on heat

for his auto   biography   he offered   a bibliography

hearing 'em write   splitting   follicles   from scalps

street code   crabs   interviews   slop

reflection   flecks   backed up   by   last night

waves tickle   nature returns something that was never ours

they write about   they write as if quail dust was a pure malt

repellant   host   missing word found safely asleep

in   the dictionary   but to hear them talk you'd   think

4: the Inches ~~the Pence~~ the Changes

4:1

waiting   get consecrated waiting   character box

hardened   like an animal   pulp   animal's pupil

waiting   *like* eternity   children's hour   so-so

we used to watch Neighbours as a family   sinking in chairs

the deserted furniture of the stairs   disgorged

a fashion   in wind/s   in slope/s   domestic frenzy

always smaller and smaller areas   of soft or hard water

drummer's song sung *like* eternity in a film of (but not for) adults

still waiting   plastic mud   holy communion kit

a movement   in the bushes   a fox the size of a bird

careless sacrifice   foxes   us   less   and   less

disgorged   not   discouraged   unlike fox sized bird

4:2

nest lens   curling box   wind trapped in Russian doll

D Day beach   unlocked hide   museum of light

sculptor regards maquette's will to live   his little paupers

stunned fever   loaded wind   weave   boulders

photo curls   fades   parades   hard data

private   beach   cast   litter   unfold

plot   unfold   stacked   letter   mime

let's climb cliffs   any cliffs?   those Dravidic cliffs!

water pistol   squash   squash in the water pistol

raid their nuts   crack those nuts   cardboard philosophies

you can't camp here   but you can make your   pitch

doll wears a glass mask heaving in&out of electromagnetic interval

4:3

such a small ghost   about the size of a grey pencil

star stoker   *land waster*   banner   a tiny year

the field slopes down towards its own shadow   unopened

cities exchange   skyscrapers   estranged sky scraps

such a small ghost   about the colour of a rule   book

degrees of sticky Viking   ink angels   Vivian   girls

the hill slopes down towards its own shadow   opened   up

twisting   margin   unclaimed   lines &   guests

the class register was huge that day   millions of children

were registered to that class that day   long long after that day

the teacher was/is still calling out   their cider pressed names

Stairwell   Margin here   Stairwell?   Imagined here Stairwell???

4:4

mending the mud   mending the broken morning   be

brief   mend the red anchor   mend the briefcase

mud   pond   bonding   breeze

torn mud   torn pond   oiled desk   amended   universe

for a brief moment there   atoms thought   they were

the lovers sift the endless void through their rather lovely reef

for the briefest of moments there   slipped   glance

dumb   purple   beyond   purple   erupt

lovely star   lovely sea   lovely star of the sea   mud

brief star   brief sea   interred   purple skin of mud

mud holes in lace interrupted by socks   underwear holes in water

water holes   mending holes in souls   in brief   songs

4:5

he breezes in   she breezes   blunder few wishes

too late   to be a native   American   Berrigan

does a caterpillar hate itself so much   that it forgets to bring

forth   actually that elephant   is moving pretty fast

she breezes out   crucifixion   revolutionary   or not

the sea comes back in   the hermits sing   *Transmission*

huge chandelier over Manchester   to be a pilgrim

glum pyrotechnics   revolutionary   or not   fun

enough fun   crucifixion   breezing   in and   out

with the tide   too late and too early   like the tide

butterfly forth   the ship comes in bringing the clouds with it

queer star   queer star turn   furtive applause   in time

4:6

involves   study   leg work   weekends

involves   quiet time   filling shoes   recording

trash   register   sublime crumpets   crumpled up sun

it will involve   bouncy haloes   gnashing fangs

the only record we have of this is absent minded leisure narrative

involves   tomorrow's contaminated borders

involves   pink boiled mouths   missed sockets

paper sun   ballet   membrane   epic foibles

unloved ash resolves streetlights on the lyric sea   of milk

the hypothetical hush   sublime shopping   sea spray

involving   celebrity forests and estuaries

read into   read right in   no   further

4:7

promise   hello   saying contact   with the walls

morris dancing in hell   stay in contract with outlaw

the gift becoming   in time   the string that ties the gift

drafting   common greeting   line and   field

which is safer at night   the woods or the park   ?

Faustian compromise   amid labial melody spill

promise   hale   pretending to search with whistle

missionary   anthropologist   apologist   leopard

the fig tree gets up a head   of steam   studio team

mistaken   ~~faces~~ bodies   the floor used as a metaphor

toby jug made of morris dancing meat   traction engine

surprised you kept it   looking forward to future   fictions

4:8

volume matters when liquid randomly moves a homemade groyne

a stub of volume   the randy sea   the habit of writing

the habit of sea   two things to talk about   table &   tennis

mattery thought   the random tactic   moving through grace

a liver like cheese   many kinds of cheating allowed in races

suddenly the difficult at first task   far too easy to see through

a groin symmetry   a   symmetrically unlawful silence

filtered   style   weak   br   id   ge

tidbits   but i always said titbits   and i still want to

coming in on waves of doomed dream   the viscous ridge of sway

spray too   don't forget spray   spray   fits

stiff flumes of clumsy god drop   last habits and   functions

4:9

gallery   the gallery tries to say something   about itself

gallery   the gallery gets up early to get itself ready for itself

dining room   hope   chestnuts   door shoots itself

i've been doing research on the typewriter on the typewriter itself

gallery   another gallery   made with a burden of suitcases

in this gallery   Sunday wardrobe   dress made by typeset

dining room   another rally round   more   rooms

caterpillar   caterpillar stations of the cross   more   or less

catalogue   comment   an exhibition   of banned books

bad tempered gallstone   on display   door finally shuts itself

gallery   of hawking teds   heavy hang the doors

military spiders   the light in the gallery   put away

4:10

transfer   darker knowledge   sacred   sarcasm

transfer   so far   lymph acrid   generous quanta

Norwegianly   provincial   Fiordly   absolute

beckon   to England   beacon   bacon   bespoken

spiral twitch   psychology   of   aggressive young monastery

vale   of   deception   slips in a reserve absolution

"absolutely"   *"absolutely"*   transfer?   *"absolutely"*

a beautiful shelter is called a bower   careless   switch

under white   under white where the shadows settle in layers

trans   parent   protractor   oblique   angle poise

sun white   net   the court follow the deer to the reservoir

the court drink *of* the water   deer discuss the cycle of mistresses

4:11

vernacular toolbox   it does what it doesn't say   it does

banknote spotted the man who was about to pick it up in poked dots

ambrosia   tinned   it wants to do what it says on the   lid

planet of sawdust   saw what was coming   in an omelette

aerodynamic mountain   father of all   hires a speech

earth buckles and shakes   but the buildings   are one big futon

reinforcements are sent in   shaking   lesbian eggs

then which is the dismal art?   evidence   they saw it coming

aisles   flanks   aisles   discrete   plumbing

swollen ladders   woollen step ladders   fermenting tools

misty mountain poets   hiding   in a tray of   hot dogs

what do the gods eat?   why   us of course   why ask?

4:12

wearing a fence around the neck instead of a necklace a neckfence

ideogram for   effort   ideogram for   masonry

exiled   by the emperor   to busy border   crossing

wearing a thread of crow intestines   instead of a wristwatch

adjusted   victims wander off in different   directions

call them back get them back here now   mountain pass

unicorn   dragon   griffin   manticore

extraction   ideogram   index   manicure

heavy back   in the absence of any elements i don't see how

that little cupcake business is a gold mine   daft stopping here

facsimile   spinal loin   that gold mine is money down the drain

grilled unicorn   a penny for these thoughts is a bargain

5: the Steps the Stars

5:1

no colour   rainbow spin re   commend shuddering

screaming gusts   inherited   anaesthetics

number paralysis   inherits tight to legal limit ethics

illicit farm udder coronation   cannon fodder in the ear

the moon turns on a hinge   earth only interested in its own

mysteries   of no colour   spun bodies of grease

the earth turns on a hinge   the moon's only newspaper

nuptial hour   ruptures shade   base   data

inflate   accelerate   sable   spectra

curtains from the shoulder   paralyse no moon   lady razor

more tugboat than spaceship   relationship 's   intervals

scheming human farm animals   like a useless insight

5:2

thankyou you interrupted by the new

honesty degrades into alien honey new nature

the trees the strength of bees deflected

defaced tree props up bat pop-up gravestones

thanks too the interested make automatic corrections

disconnected erection un relenting water flame

un more un mechanical un destroys bridge

in unAmerica be quite unclear pay your self

thanks a lot for that self in particles pure Fluxus

measured by arcane radio deal calculus a ripe 'n

neutral envelope of air guitar h.p. novelty

the tonight bees interrupted by the tablet's insurrection

5:3

descend   pretext   halt within   gentility

pretext   ransom   don't   hesitate lightly

ransom   rash   moist device   daft as a

rash   official   company car   share

officially   sick   synthetic meltwater   rift

sick chemise   skim   converging   saturation

mix up between hospital and hospice   a slick   rift

descend up   ascend down   don't   drift

rope ladder   stars in the sump   black water moon

prefixes and suffixes swimming around   in tadpole abandon

champaign revolutionary searches for a right question to ask

pretext   scree   pocket dictionary mixed into cream swill

5:4

driven to posture   driven out rushed   of warm realm

riven in post   hive   rival   beatitude

post viral   livid intuition   of warm realm

beat government   takes on   revival   flush

beautifully private   (   )toobeautiful   afterthought

doppelganger in the   middle   distance

caravan's prison cinema   projects   onto a dried flower

the enemy warns us   it is going to   attack next weak

coaxing the shooting star into the bottle   with faith support

faith supporters elusively putting out fires down the leanest plughole

mealworms   manageable pieces   of love

tiny prisons   sub-post office   stubs   vents

5:5

collector without portfolio   drains film   cool

speaking drain   acclimatized   cage rust

collection stole itself   into the cold night's control

arts' officer   luckily gets reading claustrophobia

pleated   barrier   spring   baptism

luck   good luck   bad luck   funnel

twin débuts   drained luck   drained cool from look

rusty lane   pull   the mat from under immune blends

works for you   works for us   files   for it

drives for us   drives for you   Edwardian   drives

bed control   stigmatized dance   rating seizes opportunist

rusting crate of kelp   collector's old luck   returns

5:6

sin bin spiritually curls   around what dreams are   made of

curlew   spotting curlews in poems is a sin   without motive

plumber looms over pipes   lurks   indented in Eden

myopic   lumberjack's safety first basin haircut is dangerous

trowel stew   stewed rowel   lewd bird   elevation

thousands of hundreds of tens and base units castle without motive

suppository   bullet   standing stone   iris

crow curlew   blue tit   great rock moat skirl brew iris

dip pipit blue cloud fluffy clock lure   what dreams are REALLY made

of   stewed plumber   lime scale   target   short cut

pillar of salt turned into Brookside Close

the Chapel of Ponds in   a Church of Wild   Edens

5:7

periphery   *must haves*   pole-vaulter

valuable conceit   tadpole   one who trades   in values

oxbow lake   velour   piffle   effervescence

on the edge of   your seat   on top of   the world

undercut   smash and grab   lifted   value pack

for ever and a day   converted   fitted   antique blueprint

got an ed ache   yes you must have   social science

pot of gold   sausage and mash   shame   assuaged

headland   still   terrified   vis-à-vis   Vikings

little village a little inland from Little Sea in very silent movie

Tudors   lit up the borders   with some *must haves*

peripheral thrift   verified   provenance of athlete's vest

5:8

animal discourse   humbles   blood white   resource

shuffle   bargain discourse   tight bond   huff

full on   discourse   thorough bred   im   pediment

minimal history   ramble   compete   in a huff about

graceful mess   self interest sameness   travel

scouting discourse   cutest lever tucked inside a real treat

tears   that's tears not tears   as at   bedtime

it's raining dimples and freckles they fall from the flash bang sky

condemned   amid   sea battle roses   cistern

horses for   discourses   ~~m~~aim   rattling orchids

blood press   diamonds of grapefruit   beau   brummelled

blood rose flannel   sponge ambles off site

5:9

escape from landscape illuminated off   daisy throat

scratchy slip slides off catchy coming in nanosecond   horse

basics crowd together creating a darkness   between 'em

elevator down   basement   of soft parts

destroying everything personal to you we are not being personal

bowl of trembling chicks   overflow   squashed arts

administrator knows many languages   but not this one

smacked blossom   legs blossom   dry ~~birth~~ run

escape to off & get out yer claws   lawn low litre paws

a signed device   left stage left   anchored to pink dawn

floating castle king's   west country in-laws   frost

twas shyness made outlaw's royal thirst   lazy rosy pollen

5:10

solo blanco   livid janbo   harp   sprat

practise   evil banjo   harp on   piranha

Wallace Collection   wasn't something called that?   alive or

key frightened of the hand   *practicing*   in the dark

the white evil takes on abstract wisdom   foreshortened width

Rimbaud   transplanted orifice   hallucinating

sheriff's badge   marble shack shivering efflorescence

river consults horoscope to see how much longer limbo lasts

disco   chronicle   larva   pillowcase

the coast not as a border but as a container   vacant

variety of musical instruments parked like harpoons   in the car park

tailor's dummy   baby's dummy   trunk full of odd wings

5:11

point to   the word waiting on every page for its cronies

deposit   host right in front of you   some phrase or   other

anoint   brand   pin   brand

milky stare   asterisk   bricked up glacier   gland

field   pinpoint waits   in the back of England

lifeguard   queue   practical joke   sand

a field waiting around every   pet   tactic

all the oiks   innovative rakes   pig familiar   after risk

waiting to be on cue   regulated soul distress   ghost lost

deposit   rescue what's deft in front of you   an other or

pig berg   sub   merge   Japan   pig point

branded   moss   factory   all night locked in changing room

5:12

the first plants were frustrated stalkers   few words   were used

the first hot words could dry wet sand   super words were used

no anger   the word anger   wasn't used   as usual

no regret   the word regret   pointed the wrong way   anyhow

no regrets   either   or   éclair dropped on the shop floor

yes when one word started to follow another   nobody moved

frustrating   a dry martini is never quite dry enough   psalm

the road to Totness   no longer goes to town

similarly   the parcel arrives too early to be real   psalm

opening this untrue package   is an art in   itself

lunar channels   carpet made of beetle dung   used once

stars remember us   looking down at the stars

6: the Tenets the Twists

6:1

because there was   bottle green anger   lightly rigged

or was there a because?   a fedora made of ash   lifted

jaunty donkey   dripping from   kingfisher   lips

because there were   house numbers   but no street

corridor twisted in nature's kaleidoscope remains bureaucratic

a whirlpool of spaniel tails   and other granddaddy stories

spirals of ice cream putty   ratchet   jig

because there was   lush slither   transparent jigsaw

coalmine cut out of doorway   fingernails of bottle green glass

smoke rigid   from tight fitting   yellow donkey in street

because there   dripping into shadows   another's

cut   memory   of   another's   mem~~ory~~e

6:2

musical scrag end   squad's leg end   shadow   popette

painted musical crag and   legend   of   educated gelding

legation of muses   negative white   cave light

butcher dehydrates muse   underworld   members only

empty frame   full of suffocating black stone

shadow squeezed into shadow   attempting to be the wild flower

passerby   expressionist squaddy mattress   milestone stone

wayside   millstone stone   scholar   wallflower

the pub is as   quiet as a   dead next-door   neighbour

everyone talking   at once   you can't   hear a thing

motorcycle brag   over   heard   gagging paper round

butcher's bicycle   tender to   quadruple   now there's a thing

6:3

guild of eye-witnesses discord   pains   just kidding

occult lust   jujitsu   urge to   elect intimidator

occult core   euphoric excuse   ductile gloat

guild of animators   disparity   duel homelands   hulk

gulag   *goolang goolang*   hanging paper curtains

hanging   judge   judo   judge   fudge

lurking   on a long   leash

occult curdle   euphoric jargon   justice kidding

you get what you   reserve   jacking it in   stubbornly

a classical scene   lambs' nymphs   shepherds' ~~dgo~~gds

a pastoral gulag   doggedly *be bop a loola a wam bam boom*

nightwear and wreckage   detuned   do-gooder

6:4

coral   lachrymose coral   hot metal   peppering

choral   teaching class   struggle   &   lance

they want an oeuvre   a united span   a latent   spirit

they don't get it   yet straddle   plastic that rusts

re   mind   these generalisations have no place to settle

re   ad   the compass   change   is   timeless

due   north   an hour   ago at least

news vendor sells the masonic streets   to the theatre of byways

poison chemicals gave the pea green pool   its deep blue feeling

leafing through sea horse nursery Lorca   Lorca's   eye browse

the bomb was ill   air-sick   sea-sick   they took it home

lifting it carefully from hold to locker   as if it was ᵃrare ~~coral~~ coffin

6:5

burr stew   at prime time   never think of gold as a metal

one of many panes of glass   prone on the bug-eyed ground

taboo   inlet   leafy basilica   trees injected w

lysergic acid   want to jump off the viaduct   as we do

gold   golden   golden gas   thick daylight

golden stew   rave   heraldic   via   bought music

bought words   some favourites   in there   new'uns

music gets trapped in the dense fur   and stays   in there

the border is incomplete   they are still building the fields

they are supposed to be naked in the street   on Coronation St.

at prime time   squinting   homeless under a roof of amnesia

alchemical   reverse   **flickflickereringing**   pet phoenix

6:6

mid   ocean   mid-ocean   midocean   seduction

reptile   inherited   salt mama   induction

ocean   mist   ocean missed being   re juiced

reptilian   haul   the whole country meditates   solid

stolid skin wall   deep well of skin   huge lid

choose an improvement   improvised suffering   yellow

soft velvet scream   soft velvety scream   patient mildew

soft velvety scream wins the competition   as mist lifts

latest mama   hall of dancing shawls   shoal of arrows

reprehensible in sleep   yellow sheep licks the asphalt

prophet exhibited   in zoo   about to be   closed

down   mid speech   snotty dawn

6:7

socializing with the most elemental streams of moved moment

embrace   abolish   ballet   lament moment

continental brook   brooking   polished streams

got talked into drawing   a dancers' spat in an abattoir

stumbling innocently into   the innocently imperfect

scent   sent   off   to stand on a   spot

tapped   for rent   in perfect   grammar

menial reams   got to ~~eat~~ write something

i've seen crumbs openly socializing with the smells on the table

then flicking society onto the floor without drawing any lesson

for some complicated yet simple reason they don't have a cent

one   close   magnetic   crumb

6:8

bony cold water   nipped to the   child's garland of verbs

when the cold water swam into the cold sea leaning dizzily forward

stone trees   boat pinned on the horizon   tightrope

terrace bar   veranda carpet   depopulated   canvas

now stand back   and look   overseas   drugged dinghy

harbour wall matures   now stand back   let detail dissolve

dinghy filled with psychoanalyses   shrunken water pleasure

orchestra turned ice to steam in vast movie scene

tone   toned   tan   tanned   tune   tuned   bitten

nicked metal   nicked towels   vegan and loutish with it

grandfather   clock   pecked garden   clean

look over   the sea   overlooking   overlooked

6:9

find a page already open at *doze*   stolen signature

lost nature ends up   in   displaced intuition

this misplaced dozen   remains   an inspiration

zipping along nicely   goodbye endless stream

so then   joke   so there   ok then discursive pillow

sliding echo   sign here then   sequential shirk

snared consciousness   quench thirst with lost marble

senseless structure   this lesser empire

found the page already closed at *doze*   DNA on stolen register

significance   found the footer hidden behind the header

heavy sigh accompanies the gentle bribe   assumed into

superfluous   magic   turns down   alley

6:10

i doubt if this is the right place   don't think this is my best suit

list of gas fires   tick off   don't behoove   jammer

still evening air   still night air   don't think for a moment

books line the oven shelves   1,000,000 two scoops

it behooves us   show us your jumps   demented winkle

police in pairs   of shoes   twinkled will to power

vanilla   expression is free   Beethoven   pistachio

admire the absent minded   for one millennium too long

note space   windjammer reversing through communal sky

waves of tissue close over   perfectly healthy note space

poppity sad burp   rural   sludge   queasy green

my collection of car numbers safe in the   sinking residue

6:11

before shore leave corruptions cast back in begotten strained seas

glowing artistic sports   punk fish in pairs of three

fifth suit of cards   a store of surf and tennis balls   outer layer

before leaving the house a marauding priest puts off to sea

seaburn   to see his sister   sticky clusters of shorthand

inner glow   miles of paving inside sister aeroplane

inner sport   bulging paths   tucked in

flies hole   washes hole   flying light with radical money

meanwhile   the stillborn story of the untold

Tous les arts ont produit des merveilles: l'art de gouverner n'a produit que des monstres

before home leave   kill as many as you can count

it happened inside a corrupt poem deep inside a form of harsh sport

6:12

edge   migrates   over here

no not over there   there's no rover in here   toy field

rivers   of gas   centre wavers   toy cows and sheep

yachts   schooners   Monopoly board raft in the Doldrums

escarpment   toy waves   science fiction under halogen

the hill is pure escapism   some help running league

we need some help over here   trying to   reassemble depths

the centre of the border resembles the solid sky   wave to Nana

the sky sags   in the midst   crew cheer their late manager

god's mum had to be thick skinned as well and ready to evaporate at any

moment   a stag against the serrated sky on a stamp

just for a   in a   won't be a   give us a   at this   in time

7: the Levels the Lost

7:1

it had better be better than language   men are ornaments

men carve man-breasts into the barrels of their wooden guns

this lot had better be better   than the extremely unusual

extreme distances   best kept at   a distance

usual rules   usual risks   explain nothing expect nothing

postage   dosage   rummage   voltage

pistol whipped   transparent   package

voyage   mineral   preamble   slippage

an advertising authority figure   women are fathers

maimed model sweet shop   synchronized ornaments

shielded   for close   classical conflict   Ian Hamilton

Finlay   the limited range of any silence

7:2

do you want it open?　　　do you want it closed?　　　stated

feeling around　　　for　　tailor made　　　　end　seat

fooling around　　　in a　made later　　　　end　seat

creatures with tongues the length　　　　of cross country trains

length　　　　of　　depth of　　lone travel writer　　over

heard　　　falling　　　on the common　　　　over

seen　　　laughing off　　　the commons　　heckling

length of England + length of seat = length of seat across England

do you want it　　　tiny and　　　interminable　　　container?

keep asking yourself　　　who is in there?　　feckless Tory

bastard　　　with your sated　　Tory flannel　　　*We are*

here when they say we will always be here　　robot carcass

7:3

legs dangle   passages entangle   scheming youth

fish   by degrees   taught   by   *complete strangers*

tulip wriggles through   gridiron   training young privet

jet stream   glittering drizzle   iron rain

sprouting machine   shallow furniture   off the scale

branch line   angle   the night shift   ossified

membrane and gland   classified   by   the youth

of Icarus   galls dangle their degrees   fish slalom through aerials

boardwalk   under corrugated sheet   mirror hefted

by skeletons & worms   youth scissors through   old water

doesn't that mean cutting through water meaning swimming

in a trance?   chance caught out by nostalgic shame?

7:4

use   wait   wait to use   lose   used meaning

used a meaning to say nothing   amazing   ending

end use   wait   use for a bit   use up   words

used up words and meanings improve the floor   space

ordinary everyday   ordinary everyday things   pace

extraordinarily hasty   extraordinary nasty and necessary

crab   waiting for the absurd   floor bird

waiting urgently   too extraordinary for   use

lecture   theatre buzz   dimples in   ceiling

cough sweet leaks bitter honey inside the choked-up shipwreck

there's also a buzz from the watery graves' sealed-up glooms

for the use of   to be used by authorized personnel only

7:5

treated   not changed   imagined   not made

treated   obstinate form   bread and butter dinosaur

learning how to make yourself   as familiar   as water

Alice fell   in   too   formulated   wonder

landmass   affirmed   an   arriviste   Alice   slandered

on   the footbridge   as well as on   Loose Women

ridiculous amount of wax on the map   fingernails and veins

painted hooves and a necklace of nipples   as well as a passport

continental drift   gossip   a girl's best   friend

extreme   outskirts   extreme   outfits   skirt around

issues   fantasise being lost on the diamond hard shoulder

revived   revealed   reviled   treating yourself cheated

7:6

pain of disappearance disappears in eternal instant   dotted

all those years of common taste in multiple edges   slack

private   admission to pool dozing off in a box of shadows

slotted   the heart is a kidney the kidney is a miniature zoo

napalm corset   clichéd   perversions

Jimi's rainbow skin   flaming roses   *the dollar hurts*

collection cap   collection plate   Jacques   Prévert's

hushed eyelids   deprecatory Picasso   respiratory

but the pain appears detached from time and space   it tots up

from the horse's mouth readymade for lip reader   tabloid

public   a ticket for summer a ticket for the golden bonfire

sparkler   admission to skinny dip inside extreme physics

7:7

men murdering each other   not murderers   immediately

accidental   breast pocket   spiritual   insurance

men murdering each other   called soldiers

nice lining   thespian   not   delayed   immediately

called   propositioned   baptized   ferrous wheel

tip   up   embarrassed   by the   distance

pitted   against   ritual   sin   peeled off

loaded   anomaly aware   nine gnome grades   of life

stance things down   two hicky moons in the sky tonight

sugar mouse cemented in   iced rice sugar   empty right side up

frivolous   insurance   waylaid   Dane law

lies   light up   eternity   but not   immediately

7:8

the buxom waters   the buxom blue waters   tarmac

sterile clarity   the dispersal of space   hydraulics

the selfless mixer   scent pattern   whale's big tears

the buxom waters   whale's tiny steps   dandruff

the bald waters   hold tight to the smoke or you'll fall

past midnight   the wedding reception   still kicking off

this is one d.j. they didn't hang   scent pattern   bald sea

top and tail the dapper green man   a proper little green man

eugenic stars   there is energy in this room   i can feel it

dry   and   straight   dragged screaming into silence

that   one   is   spoken   for   and it began in

innocence   no questions asked   of the buxom blue water

7:9

weak watercolour sky thirst   local faith   feigned

first weak watercolour sea   Spartan   hallucination

spectacle feeds   local consolation   peasant   sorcery

however hard you try dawn you will never be as casual as dusk

why is your enemy as calm as stone?   outgrowing   fate

vacuum   no longer empty though   gravel burns faster

afloat on unoriginal fire   a Persian ship   pretending to

flee?   or it could be   the shadows in an empty cage

sky presses   skin tightens   migraine   ripe vision

strong oily and glistening with thirst   the last remaining sea

it's all revolting   eating our own opinions   feigned

weak echo   nevertheless has the stubbornness of a curse

7:10

a liquid brush   with synchronicity's   cold laughter

then   typhoon sentiments   mauve shadow salts

then   laws so vast   they can never be changed

an aura of imaginary statistics quits   fever's   riddles

exile buys the debt accruing on the shepherds' overdue library

tickets   he still does carnal business for the civil service

shepherds know no new stories to insure against their happiness

is it swifts or swallows that swim and dive between the banners?

giant squid   tycoon   realistic weed   the liquid brush

as mentioned   above   as repeated   above

which is the greater mystery   sentience   or non-sentience?

and umm....   is it a typhoon or a tycoon asking the question?

7:11

deserter   forest   an ancient somnambulant   pulse

creatures parade their secret fantasies past the sleeping   men

lovers escape their love   down any path that opens before them

criminal   dungeon   ancient insomnia   eternal rest

what has this acrid clown got to do with the smoke they call poetry?

tragic origins   scars   primitive practicalities

fragments in kiln   reform as   crawling tongues   licking ash

deserter sings with the birds and dies with   poisoned badgers

the latest batch arrive at the starless depot nourished by anguish

this is the little prison   it is smaller than you   deserter

and in this little prison grows an even smaller forest of dead trees

yes   this is where the dry dead ~~grow~~   brittle yet unbroken

7:12

cherry father   felt represented instead of   relayed

are you the right one to be   presented? yet   again

summer in a hurry   burrowing into those hidey holes

freedom   skill   social conscience   all get a free ride

set down with the saddest pride   always treasonable for

some reason   or   other   the nature poet returns

just as the possible commits itself   ungainly to ambiguity

equality   luck   social conscience   all pay in amber

you arrive in the village created entirely by artists but lived in by

the cherry fathers   it is late   no children sleep here

liberty   aromatic orgy   social worker treason   all

tremble so hard and so fast the village disintegrates around them

8: the Tribes ~~the Titles~~ the Tricks

8:1

there will never be time   there never was   time

years awarding themselves all the prizes leave nothing instrumental

maybe time is crystallized absence   though more likely it's a

geometric balance   between   different peaks of language

demonstration   do we see more through a broken window?

compare *The Lives of the Saints* with *The Life and Times of Frosty the*

Snowman   we could say no comparison   not this   time

birds   gooey air   time's birds   scatter

take any two writers sit them down and eventually they'll be writing

the same thing   there will never be enough time for this not

to happen   the poor are never with us that's the problem

birds   quiz birds   quislings   goslings

8:2

scouting   scooting   or   coming back for more fate

play for radio in which mod revivalists foster a motorbike   as if

radio could show off like that   spectator sport   moved on

to repeated demands for repeats   it's science   simple

vintage car rally at a ruined mansion and Roy Fisher walkingsticks

by   pretty sure it wasn't him as much as it looked like him

Jaguar   Austin Healey   popcorn   The Hairy Bikers

though pretty sure it wasn't them as much as it looked like   them

chchimneyswsweep brbrushes sprsprouting from an unwashed spine

dripping jewels replaced by the chasms from which they were ripped

hanging chasms stolen from no qualms by a man all principled in black

back for more   scaffolding around folly made of sardonic tubes

8:3

that *deaf dumb and blind kid* is mean with his encrypted defenses

bailiff   references   numbly resigned to human kindness

we could play with him   call him Bay Leaf   laugh at his kind

any kindred spirit left behind is swallowed by nocturnal patience

the plot on the hill is stony and too steep   luminous shingle

sequestered goods include a stuffed seagull weeping its cries

double-gate artwork features   medieval spaceman's vomit

one who doesn't dare look at you   believes in too many of you

the silence is desperate to speak   about silence

eggs get laid on Sunday too   just as well as not being laid

so count the eggs again   from the other   end

Mary Magdalene 5716   Russian ~~spy~~ spacewoman 5688

8:4

saluting   bad medicine   accepting   compacted refuse

chiseling   powdery cliff   looting   nest

north of the north   three segments of the globe   rugby

platinum kneecaps   Cardinal Wolsey   scrubbing tool

the dump used to resemble every other filled in hole on the island

find what you threw away   found wanting in a doorway

necklace of pink and yellow bites   sculptures of Latin feet

sea   white   sky   a pale green medicine   not taken

possibilities smatter on the   sports shop window display

soldiers helping those they've shot to sit up under hair dryers

cardinal   sin   deleted   by Cardinal Richelieu   he's

as insane as a piece of   coal   as sly as arson in the   ruck

8:5

timber steaks   lumber pork   wrinkled bat tablets

what will they call you   after they have   *cut you down?*

go-cart with woolen wheels on stilts of hollow bone   keening

suffering to *Poetry Please* and screaming foot and mouth disease

landscape is blurred by an implied outline of focused definitions

horse fair   Rupert Annual insulation   or extraction

the porters have been cut out of their foulmouthed scrapbook

Beatle fringe cut into a slope   a meteorologist dragging his feet

i want to return to the horse fair   to its optimistic economics and

stare   refuel and   stare   drinking straight from a

straw tower   regaling last year's burnt-in Gaelic goodbyes

then we'll find that same spot by the river where we slept so soundly

8:6

implicated   measured   butterfly temple rain

the ego loses one of its shoulder pads   look for it in the Bible

what we own is cheap   aphorism   when sharing a campus

should cramming for RE exam mean missing out on other cramps?

the cruelty of the ballad is not being cruel to be a kind aphorism

you are still implicated   live with it   heretic   tick it

chameleon drools in anticipation   of physical histories

eternity should be arranged in alphabetical   order/s

honesty cleans out the aquarium hyperbole fills it with castle weed

the room itself is like an aquarium   you drift in and   out

i can't breathe in here   i can only try to   count the colours

why's everyone got it in for Richard Dawkins' coloured shadows?

8:7

fragile   recently the antiquarian has shown signs of madness

focus   group   suffocate in four-poster   sick bag

the need to get out and about   the air is a free gallon of kisses

rabbit   dainty   road movie   free   of guns

you will never make it in those estates of free kisses   lupine

lonely one   loyal patriot of a country smaller than your bathroom

well if Jesus can live in that tabernacle i can get by in this soap dish

other by&by's include dour roads patrolled by careerist maniacs etc.

gossip   terrace   androgynous   fake   taste

vacillating   between   mental ~~arithmetic   and~~   illness

and   selling my cigarette cards on eBay singing *That'll be the Day*

as   the wind vacillates between a stone circle and a bandy tree

8:8

heel   thorn   leech   half-day   closing

white bull   unburdened of Europa's   grip/es

crossing   the vegetable stews   of lowly Doggerland

stock taking   in a   horizontal avalanche   of cheese

harsh farms   golfing farmland   half-day   healing

henchman   grabbing   horns   clenching   thorns

hunter gatherer   gathers bottles   hunts for   gripe water

down at   a clean pair of   *step we gaily on we go*

where the wall of water clots and congeals   squeezing time

the white bull is overtaken by the discontinuity of white horses

aphrodisiac   for postmodernists only   those tourists

the chateaux is closed but feel free to walk around the walled garden

8:9

believe in these weather conditions   reduced architectures

can you spare   one of those   spare   stones?

yes pace up and down but are you counting   space or time?

light doesn't travel well   emotionally it remains in its parish

this moor is a unique analogy   the smallest possible myth

without me   with a rage of bees   on a pear

pheasants   artists' models   to   share

peacock's display   slate cathedral   spare buck

pimp finds himself frozen in a monochrome concrete   poem

die in your own spare time   parasite   straight talking

believe in these cash points of nature these monumental gizzards

final replay   donkey pins tail on the meditating lizard

8:10

abandoned shoe on the steps of the city hall   video beggar

lost slipper on the steps of the museum   desire advertises it

broken high-heel on the steps of the library   queen rain

night feels its way around the shapes   sandal of unfastened light

sound picture given by the word   foliage   has its uses

late horror film plays itself down   cistern blocks with sulfur

in a ghost's world the universe is white therefore the stars are black

baroque engine shakes a spider from the shoe   black noise

my computer calls all my poems documents   the dice is loaded

lost documents nag   as if they were obsolete skills

yet   an aesthete steals crisp foreskins from the cutting room floor

twins   identical twins   slippery steps   queen rain

8:11

sirens   mermaid deception bombs   brass parrot

rubbing   life's work imagined   baby seal social climber

butter   buying publicity   desiring monotonous company

better   go back for breakfast without discussing it first

the siren pulls herself   up the rock   weds police officer

a genius in the kitchen   armadillo soup   wren broth

Mills&Boon piss artist   uses   *gasmask* and *sponge*

throbbing wren   an epidemic of topical wit   a little misery

man from audience wants us to talk about the enigma of Roy Orbison

mermaid buttonholes me at both black mass and the air raid club

all those sent out to *get a life* come back later outdated and   smug

i've got the dilettanti blues hearing a dilettanti sing   the blues

8:12

bleak   those who hate it and those who love it   call it

so what does this mean   word?   the bleak   quarry

shortly after saying it you leave it   the white   memory

on bleak Portland we had so few days with trees in them that we

possessive apostrophes   the property ladder   bleak out

look   cute misuse   dropout's ghost in cement mixer

anybody use *any* anymore anyway?   the real dropout would be

one who dropped out of   language   listen and   ~~learn~~

teak mahogany   only when there is   such a thing   but

language lea

          ks   which is why I think Freud was onto something

on leaky Portland we had so few nights without limestone that we

9: the Signs the S~~y~~stems

9:1

language left to do its own thing   remains as loyal as a good dog

experience has its own shadow yet there are exceptions to every

living thing in _____ limbo

dancer   nomadic   eye collector   deep space lagoon

your smile will be rewarded with a better world than the one at

which you smile   your dance will be rewarded with a

better world than the one you dance   ~~for in upon~~   around

left   to its own   devices   weir breaks the water into light

hand luggage   suffers caress   supernova breeds

disloyal   ceremony   in the eye collector's still pond

the missing words are never found they've never even

been substitutes   odd little numbers   invading the pitch

9:2

seal	lease	easel	fasten	your
draw	in	copy yourself	raw	
warden	air raid	traffic	Arden	war
gentle waves	gentle	shoreline	gentle feet	

white light from slim yellow lamps glows thin in the black silence

there should only be one lamp   and it should be a red hot coal

that death is not silent you can hear it's waves rising to heaven

these waves are copying each other breaking free of our gravity

madness	therapy	the breeze	composed	like soil
imagine being mad and at the end of the universe			yourself	
energy saving candle	sputters on	late	lesson	
submarine	pen	submarine pen	sleaze	

9:3

open fruit of the leg   touch glass   soft knee   pip

arms of delirium   embrace cartilage   body search

opaque   gristle   snaps brace   instant wandering

an apparition of hard labour   adders where grass lifts stones

the sea is stitched   the cliff zipped   medical museum

breath   caves in   lake in the crater   back lane

opening sperm's   anecdotal permanence   under glass

concubine fixes her hair with   cramped vertigo

the attempt to split poetry into two   fails   two thieves

two types   of inhibition   inference fruit   tripe pie

sleeping languages beautiful in their caskets   w i n k s l o w l y

gladiator fights gridlock with a chrome net of   mirroring shrapnel

9:4

skinless Mini   Cooper   recruiting bulky elderly kin

barely glimpsed thrusting an arm through the ~~sidewalk~~ handcuff

hotplate   template   tall man in a tall   rusting city

dwarfed hot dog seller   latest dwarf dog   rusted cogs

growing into mortality   abstract church   wharf design

scale model mortality   cathedral tract   Gestapo tact

psycho geographer   splashes out   on a leather coat

it WAS the future   a long piss on the bus schedule's thin skin

the countryside is god incarnate   sleeping through all readings

it's come so far   to be here at all   miniature monster

you wanted words to stand alone   to be embarrassed in your place

where is the skin now   of the skinned zebra?   Abbey Rd.

9:5

modest verve   how many e's in Ashbery?   votive reader

the ladders are not ladders   of ambition   but

borrowings from someone else's weather   it's a grim job

scratching   all the simultaneous   itches

lice and angels   the dissolution   of the laboratories

space dust   there is an underground station here some

where   a beautiful and monstrous antidote   to suicide

for the homeless beast   the recluse   incomplete in the crowd

then the simultaneous itches become nebulas of abstract nouns &

drunken hell ignites after eons of   waiting   for to

morrow   melting   celebrity wax &   Wayne   &

Waynetta sat on damp car seat in Baker St. electricity sub station

9:6

small arms   bypass   postmodern folk memory   pub

we didn't go on a bender we went on a small parabolic   wander

alcohol goes well with philosophy   with exposure too

without witnesses   an anti-mark   mute bungle

giraffe takes in the small night air   licks a few stars from the sky

Leonora Carrington kept a baby giraffe as a pony   apparently

rocking chair had a bad back for a parent grammar   reluctantly

horse climbs the stairs   to Berkshire   it's a   detour

light readers are usually heavy sleepers   without evidence

baseline   in search of the mummified tune the dealer hums

a bit extortionate for what is   after all   a small exorcism

stamp collection   antibody   water hole etiquette

9:7

lunar slush   tidal bore   guard's van   adrift

tasting scent   tidal lips   tongue guard   drift

a complex tax   e.g.   a tax on complexity rift

the cawing of the mad rooks   adjacent   in the mad trees

lunar runnels   idle bore   Bluebeard's homemade   jam

a fresh start   white lies   jellyfish   spread   over

spill   a vessel of dull sparks   laconic   colony

the soul is an old potato sack   carrying a heavy glutinous slop

zephyr   fusion of insomnia and dense sleep   lunar shush

but there is no atmosphere in here the wind is a hushed splash

tasteless scent   e.g.   a tax on ~~celebrity~~ simplicity

guard's van in flood opens its doors to rooks dreaming of damned trees

9:8

dark blue veins in the sky   half moons and   jugglers

dark blue van in rebus   half a horse race   spring

stilted jive talk   tilts   a pyramid of   gymnasts

anthropomorphic morning   a good day for   fishing

wish list   fishing for flesh and blood in the holes of the bicycle

things to do   scorpions   tack those sails clean that dais

flyweight   Amelia Pond   Jean Arp   fox

primordial fairytale   scoff   dragonfly   flail

there used to be a border here separating the human from a cult

now flightless birds have reclaimed it   by planting swing seats

dark cracks in the ~~circus~~   dark cracks in the ~~ark~~   dark cracks

in the sea   mechanical angels waltz through shaft   voluble

9:9

do you get lamp trouble?   have you got it?   whirlwind

whirlwind squint   have you got one?   hostile messenger

are you academic?   extinguished diamond   laughter line

stained glass goiter   are you an academic?   humpback

hump climbs back up   the swollen shell   electric gate

pump more silence into the geometric forms   already blushing

a spate of vandalism   dangerously close to the family   tomb

lush embarrassment   arabesque gate to an   *attraction*

are you still swinging it?   who had an album called *Schubert Dip*?

laughter line   stains   whirling soap dishes   shed

wings   saliva   against   a thousand island sunsets

lamp giving trouble gives no light   but you can smell its heat

9:10

alchemical cache   poem synthesizer   rushed art

fluid   blue   nauseous freeform swerve head

involuntary royal   trust in music   fluctuates

gentle   disarray   an abandoned   frequency

astrophysics is not a pseudo science it's an enthusiastic intervention

placebo   disarray   cassette   of cerebral pornography

Passchendaele = a shepherd's vengeance   studio chemistry

forgets   what   comes   next

oh yes emerges   a Madonna of displeasure   a hornet

dog's pills belong to me   officially my   pre-programmed

innovation   shuffling those favourite old ~~flavours~~ futures

with derisory   history   OFFICIAL NAZI PARTY ASTRO   LOGER

9:11

at laughter falls effortless traveler east creeps west

closed eyes   held breath ever thought of

moving magnetized crumbs by hand along random

margins water leveler falls in with the slow baking crowd

the novel a simulation the inevitable a voyage

industrial industrial scale envy drawn and repulsed

fingernail torrent rock jelly nature's shop front

pretty trade samples wrapped in an ocean of skuas' jabbing steel

the final miles of the marathon are either the hardest or the easiest

i'd imagine Maid Marion brown and pale

the river entered the forest but i haven't seen it come out yet

imagine what is going on in there all that zen cake and ale laughter

9:12

gone   gone   over

saddles   hurdles   hearses   keys hang   over/s

stadium   horses   conjurers   blinkers   gone

over   open ground   impressions and   melds

windows in all those languages   all the stolen languages

neurons bunch together   strangers who want to eat your hair

all gone   hollow ground   waiting room door finally opens

dogs carrying luggage   evening walk into endless night

alien half gift   guitar effulgence   showering in horse box

lost steam   the poetry of the streets swept up and burnt

i've been a rover for many a year   says the shopkeeper

no good   gone   unable to wish you will ever be born

10: the Labours the Lonely

10:1

page 1 of 1   words 5 of 7   words 9 of 12   track

page 1 of 1   words 18 of 20   words 22 of 24   track

print layout view   loveliness   unloved   track

page 1 of 1   words 36 of 38   whispering   eyes

vestige   public space empty   opera and   mime

trampoline carried onto the stage   rehearsed psychosomatics

the pregnant maneuver   takes longer than a stewed pause

rage 1 of 0   words 70 of 72   tracer fire   self taught

once wrote a poem about David Bowie on a piece of greaseproof paper

i was working in a burger van   rating   half an explanation

metaphysical art caught moody fish dressed in drunken sailor's cap

a violence of suspenders in lexical rhythm   extreme   retina

10:2

broken record   presentiment born as a broken   record

raven   raven in the fridge   grebe coated in anti-freeze

skull born   presentiment as a broken   record

raven   its body made of the dead   spirit of feathers

never dirty again   the Hoover has 7 points to choose from

raven sucks up the remains of the pond   through an hour glass

look at you   covered in broken records   it's a record

emus   ravenous at the fridge   and not for plums

haven is   interrupted   by a cold call concerning solar panels

these are Welsh but the sun is run by the   English gob gov.

Irish rapper grabs your tail   your fate   amuses strangers

Scotch lacquer drying under awning   token record   token

10:3

this is the scenery that exhausts the tourist   close your eyes

close your eyes tired tourist   sleep   you are on holiday

the change in scenery catches up with all of us   we are creations

stagehands migrate   out of impatience   we are creators

sleeping in a tray of chemicals   ~~out on strike out~~ out of stock

abstraction   of desire   idiotic   with promise

orchestra   behind the scenery   dress suit and dickied

manic film music wakes the film extras by unfolding their ears

daily printer   poison finger probes mind   problem

snobs slob about in capitalism's slop tray   an appeal for wit

nesses   from the bobbing classes   but i never saw a thing

i was window shopping officer for any reflection looking like me

10:4

outside there are degrees in rhetorical gardens   unawares

out there   space paces itself in   space   hardware

baby gull selling Big Issue processes summer inside a distressed

greatcoat   but it's sleigh bell bodice that gets the cup of tea

hawks in wall cavity sing *a line of hills over there must be a plateau*

which way are we now facing?   facing-off a superstition of mirrors

metallic country walk through static sulks mentally ticky-tacked

naughty boy is going nowhere   staying   nowhere native

ought there to be grades in glade collections   escaped off

landgirls   overtaking an   undertaker   unbrothered

don't burn the church down boys but burn the air   out of it

which way are we facing now?   sparks of wistful   blessing

10:5

meeting Steve   in the Gog and Magog   on Curry Thursday

orphaned expressionism   tabulated   herb infection

teeming up   with   bugged table   Wetherspoons

talk cannot be avoided like trying   *not to chew fruit pastille*

these are the deserted docks that tv cops come to to swop prisoners

under a vagabond moon   a spoonful of soul   highlights a chin

container lorries   buggering off to Birmingham   stacked odds

director decided his adaptation of Beowulf would be in modern dress

stags   talking back in Catalan   something to remember to

talk about   flailing about in a spoonful of dust   can it be

we're too fond of humour   to   explore   with convict

ion?   trophy heads of flies and spiders stuffed with honey

10:6

discrete   duplicator   flatterer   extinct reason

layers of razor   scare off the voyeur   7 Gorge Terrace

letter stagnates before it is finished   ambassador ambushed

the victim of a teacher's anger   reflects on the   future

scars without a history   queue at the copier   siege breaker

fumes from the anger   snag on the handle   wood turner

before it was a beach it was a counterfeiter's stash of origami paper

pool table has versions called pinball waterbed &   bagatelle

he was a student of literature but could only do anagrams by cheating

he was a poet but could only get cryptic clues by secretly smelting

lotus bed suspense   pull back the plunger and re   lease

(baguette poked under statue's arm)   (moustache drawn on lady)

10:7

we found the grave on the 7th floor   it looked like a drinks

machine   i wonder what the body looks like now i remarked

to mum   i think the body must look like drinks i   added

she was genuinely shocked she turned us both into guilty parties

another day in this *immortal combat* i tried to engage her in con

versation about Death and Spain but we only got as far as Ireland

wasps   vicious ~~Irish~~ Spanish wasps and tame ~~Spanish~~ Irish

bulls   no cars   dappled sunlight   avenue to the lake

rose   Rose   arterioles in the rowdy summer flower

the delicate mechanism inside the drinks machine   kicks in

students ejaculating in the library   oversubscribed choices

we found the elevator hiding in the pale stairwell   looking green

10:8

beach umbra   umbrella each   shop dummy storm front

indentured whimsy   coffin dope idyllic kitsch cycle

jettisoned squeal aura   soft rock   robot gone   feral

however stiff   rip it from its   knees to ship's   bell

buried with his special effects   + at least 1 favourite assistant

as a memory aid   + a list of addresses   which he will cull

down to   absolute zero   + a rapid response inflammable

fire boat   to searchlight the silky seas of fire   for hope

hope's sequel   static tingle   every touch   a sting of

hot ice   psychedelic lo-fi   flying saucer humiliation

getting warmer   in the winter sea   cold   sweat

beach towel   return to your cupboard   to your synaesthetic lair

10:9

alumni   economy is easy to believe but hard to understand

beauty is hard to believe but easy to understand   Tourettes

mid August and i'm still singing carols   and saying *tubular bells*

flocks of moths cometh   summer school murders on tv

boredom works the same way as pain you have to break its barrier

like this: like this   like this   and   like this

pelvic sandstone range   on sale with marionettes' original sin

sleep is only days away   yet death is   minutes off

comet is not a celestial body it is a medal   leaden soubrette

unwrap your medals sometimes   to fiddle with pride and tinker

spy   one of your medals is a comet in the vaginal night

like this furtive decoration reunited with tin butterfly's pin number

10:10

puffing down the mountain   to make covert music in the trees

dawn puffs up the little hill   to get a grip on middle England

remission   hair-of-the-dog   ecstatic and expansive lay-in

the tight vibrations of poesy   loosening   concentration

concertina squeezes space   before fanning the note   out

but what will happen to the tone   when   the   tabs   are

s   c   r   a   m   b   l   e   d?

will daylight still slip down the mountain to hibernate in the sea?

joy channel   cramped juice   Charleville   ramble

coy runnel   bled grace   drained   etymologist

my Uncle Ted had a trial for Spurs   John Hall came out of Africa

but will i fall   awake   to sleepwalk such a shiny world?

10:11

sand panda tachisme   rearing north nor'east   red ace

wave stuck to the sky will never veer off flag day   to boast

surfboard graveyard   left behind   on the *blue bus*

badge: SURFERS AGAINST GOD   strands of fluffed lines

gang of white ants carry a pen along the beach behind the gallery

place it   where it is possible   to be   named

slap it down in the sand   with the other inflatable priests

and baptized parasites   back stroking   an abstract map

Freud 's not himself today   replica shark grins not unlike himself

hedgehog fish tachisme   acid test bearing south sou'west

consciousness cocktail   lashed out   at the precise moment

the bodyguard put down his Ubu Roi   to model for Guernica

10:12

thesaurus page blades   sea mistakes land for more sea

once this has happened it will always happen   this rococo dis

agreement   contracting roots entangle in contract   under

leaf raiment   aqueous meadow road   cut and ribboned

further inland there are other seas   sweet and bitter seas

these can be mistaken for sunspot threshers   fraternity

machines that copy the mistakes of man   they define us

land   tucked in   with the Faustian fears   of the sea

rotating phobias   mistake unequivocally   love's resistance

serious joy this losing business   fidelity's slot machine

the ghost in the thesaurus   agreeing to disagree or what?

we see a haunted station platform where really no really there is only

11: the Tones the Techniques

11:1

creeping across the desolate landscapes of the rim   accidently

lurid field   twisted crosses   twisted crescents

sky seams burst   lung elliptic   snails play Twister

and poker players refuse to help the children bring in the harvest

salmon courtesan dances across the desolate play of incidentals

whittled skittish   though still saddled and   anchored

snail of mountains   bubble-bath mountain gauze soufflé

driven to the whist drive   in the shell of a burnt out   car

concentric abduction   birthmark rosette   ion

puckered poster siren   sorbet axis   retrial (in writing please)

poets don't write   they just snuffle about it to themselves

they don't even talk they shuffle it and not even to themselves

11:2

rebuff   baffled   fled   into the nut fields   new radix

i've got a brand new combine Wurlitzer   but I've lost   the key

scarecrow at attention on the cathedral green   stuffed with silt

the soul is weightless it cannot be judged as if it was chewing gum

the washing has been on the line for four years, nearly five actually

rain   sun   rain   sun   rain

it just so happens that at the end of its time line it's raining again

typical   cultural   buffer   baffled   typical

they pursued the editor into the pistachio fields   an old

matrix   the book i've been reading   springs shut

at the wrong page   all detectives thus flounder and fail

anonymous   oracle   gilded   over

11:3

leaving the room   a night's work   snags on a detail

you have a photographic memory but nothing to show   for it

scene set yesterday's nature   wildlife live-feed disappointment

a shoal of birds   blind pass   a flock of badgers

tipoff   print's protocols   face extinction   bets are off

philosophers would prefer it if animals   stayed out   of the picture

stark rigid reticulation   bound to a bare rock by your tongue

while everything   living and unloving   moves around it

and the sound of my childhood sea as it shifts the great bank of stones

is transported to Euston Road by an artist   as if it was an animal

and he was   setting it free   (setting?)   all art sucks

so many metaphors are taken from it (reality) that it should be empty

11:4

brooding   dehumanised by boredom and impatience   un

true   depersonalised mini universes   obdurate spectra

offbeat riots   micro   performance   counter cult

ure   Army and Navy Stores   i'll be with you in a moment sir

a blue flame at the back of the cave   menstrual sleeping bag

a coat long and heavy enough to carry the weight of the ~~world~~ sea

upstairs   too proud to pretend to   storm the winter palace

laminated yawn   spike   pierces yawn

we have 15 minutes to get to the radio before the war starts there

in-bred resident   charismatic   executive toy

will DNA proper   withstand the pull   on its strands

of DNA as metaphor?   disembodied spin cycle

11:5

long flash   for   bidden   vanishing   shelf life

harsh cash   the human moon   Brecht's *Ballad*

of Hannah Cash   soul crushed   the human head of moon

linen fish   nylon fulcrum   frantic oral   finish~~ing~~ school

interregnum   subterranean river   aboriginal voice

second vision   following your strong letter to the authorities

up its terminal incline   watch it being screened behind   the

high altar   bicycle shed's smoker's kiss under a second moon

restoration   forgotten regret   forgotten   target

Aztec secularisation   cabin boy visits drummer boy's grave

but keeps on going on about chain letters and   pyramid selling

if moon wasn't already   an empty ballroom   he'd be dying

11:6

instead　　yet not　　accidental　　　an undertow ago

futurists' fastest rhetoric yet translated into domestic English verse

Polynesian　yet　unknown too　　　in a canoe that's not for

~~sport~~ sale　yet　Picabia's *Little Girl Valley*　up　ended

rich man likes to surround himself with abysmal representations

these representations of emptiness clutter unto the middle distance

a trick clock　~~winds you up~~　　go to your room　stay there

reality of course is neither messy nor orderly it's always a new trick

there will be　　no more　stopwatches　　to amend

that's twice this new lunatic pope has asked to be my intellectual

friend　　he outlived his bullet-proof vest　plus I'd like to

see Sweden solely through ventriloquism　　my only modernism

11:7

dusk trickles   trees follow   ripe for massacre

criminal   tickled pink   jealousy and   stairs

the portraits   impenetrable barriers to   perspective

go back outside   wedding reception   and   stairwell

twilight branches   to the left   muffled   lovers' tiff

tiff   is that a real word?   regiment fitted with right boots

leaving for circuit training   around the black universe

then breathing alone tries to open the door   tries to come in

trick dissolves mosaic   pink sun   drifts   across road

somatic crime   borrows   dusk's dry resolve

sailing ship is crewed by egg timers and captained by a blue garter

amateur night maneuvers   trickle nicks at sand castle

11:8

idle gods and busy sods simultaneously invent hermaphrodite car

idle religion   busy woman   make virtue a necessity

Dadaist formulae   anew   under oily Parisian stars

bridge   steps hung   bunch of helium balloons

fuzzy gods' in-laws the fussy muses amuse us with titular stodge

romantics confined to barracks   ephemeral   tummy ache

artist leans too far out of a window   and looks   suspicious

virgin rag-and-bones supports herself by leaning against Torso No. 9

a bird   by the way   is a tiny mathematician   a domino

overused words such as *domino* are clichés only for a   few days

snobs   in the gallery   breathe   underwater

slut naiveté   consults astrologer   (vice versa as well)

11:9

shut   shut in   shut   shut out   shout the full vision of

Aintree off course   engraved on the sun's solid gold dumbfound

darkness   engraved in the sun's soft gold   deposit

grout the full version   city sinks beneath its own height

a big adult hand conceals the door handle   the hand twists

eviction   prison   narrative respect   blinkered

child manhandles the art materials   the materials love it

to an outside observer this child is only what he manages to ride

deprived of an inner life high capitalism volunteers to lift corpses

over the wall   implanted *différance* squeezed out by a conjugal

sigh so sharp   it scythes through the preposition compound

children's high spirits build the wall from the top   down

11:10

earth's hips   earth's rudder   earth's infernal vats

jack o'lanterns   squealing   in the Vatican City Zoo

carnivorous machine cleans the streets   the dispensation of dawn

earth's cousins   Dresden   health and   safety

poets are weird people so avant-garde poets are very weird people

goes without saying   yes it would have gone without saying

rereading at 60 the books i read at 16   to close the weird circle

spinning spiv demon screws into the crust like a vernal superhero

retrace   botox kebab   retreat   shell shocked

incessant pop art   from those who went forth and   divided

refugees   film extras   ruddy undercoat   business plan

you twirl me right round baby right round   lost   earththread

11:11

deep on the summit of   love   and its breathless   poisons

trembling   water   reflecting   the inner ear

butcher's barricade of   soap   and its thoughtless aphorisms

waitress   spirited away   through a labyrinth in the air

desideratum   quoting yourself   you don't look like this

how ever many times you look back over your shoulder's   twist

immortal   wound   an open   door to   a border

that has infinite breadth but no   length   Reverdy

meanwhile   time's been decaying apposite metaphysical furniture

immortalizing those who refuse to squeeze themselves into the esc

ape tunnel   at their   physical peak   itinerant goat licks

its goat self but one day clicks away it will pilot us to the cruel stars

11:12

devote   tattoo   to   the milky way across your back

fountain   opaque   burning dust and   pronouns

station concourse glass bladder   solipsist psoriasis

plump laboratory euphemisms   degraded epiphany

red resurrection tattoo   thorn forest   strewn tacks

synaptic drain   resonance   of reborn   meat

unrecognizable when out of your uniform   of black treacle

hare buckets down   on the quiet path   beside torn tracks

article in magazine   on broken   hearted   objet d'art

waiting room is empty except one who arrives   too late to wait

changing room mimic ~~says~~ panics   *change*   *change here*

Eros builds his cathedral with peach stones and devotees' graffiti

12: the Jurors the Jesters

12:1

Lenin   after Mayakovsky   *will always*   *live*

Mayakovsky   after Lenin   will never   die

be resolute   comrades   don't let me stop you *grinding bastards*

happily posthaste high up a deep depression down the wastes of time

rascal   put on your last remaining   mystic waistcoat

your enemies are decadent and sick and won't work without reward

mind you   all this paper work is crazy   without electricity

your friends   are being far too rational   as usual

steely grammar lifts the day   fills the night with bright holes

come back   labour scamp   the flags are made of lightening

the songs are made of thunder   capitalists everywhere   beware

the constructive hooligan   cigar soaked in petrol by an artist's paw

12:2

it moves in blood moves   blood moves in black rivers

tourists   tombs   the bridges drink the city's spat blood

words erected from bits and pieces of *any old* iron   mutilators

shaking   edifices and fists   a heap of nonchalant whistling

many hands make heavy work   miracle   the bleeding wall

sap moves through a series of images   hooded letters   bile

the blackest of the black rivers rushes the university into amnesia

popular cinema is not the same creature as a painted   scaffold

incarnation   circumcision   an asymmetric butterfly

little pile of silver whistles   screaming in the golden sun

juggler drops transplant   street entertainment   single feature

tortured heart   rowing past towers   weeping statistics

12:3

terror of death is great   when   we've   had

language stuffing   spiraling   from the throat's   red well

for ever   (life backwards is always forever – no beginning)

this language fuss is the language in which death is terrible stuff

screaming whispers   howling into the echo chamber

of...   wait for it...   media studies

the muse of media studies   the devil in the cross   wires

easy target   elan crunch   *the violet man*

all literary products   poems plays novels   are short lets

like *The*   *Division*   *Bell*

or   the horror of chamber music   the eland munches

in adrenal ruins   emotionally afraid of the bureaucratic instinct

12:4

nightmares of perfection   tilting   the faintest vanity

sensual engineering   echo   of unreason   rehearsing

Dadaist footlight   tries to exit with the shadows   jostling

sweet nightmare light   plural universal   carries it off

then one day the roofer slips on his own shadow   trip lyre

sick with impatience he slaps onto the tilting tiles   familial

ecstatically he survives embarrassing death   lady luck

MOMA of perfection   climbing tackle jewelry   gesture

mind reading repair   hermetic jazz   ego in underwear

or *brain dressed in tight fitting dress*   *disclosing its real shape*

mayoral   opportune lilting   waste of a   superstition

minister of innovation in the arts also known as minister of the interior

12:5

distractions are an inadequate substitute   for everything

happening   at once   i detest the postmodern   skills

thanks for   nothing   i could frame that incestuous advice

mush   a vile rumor makes for a melancholy pre-Raphaelite to

morrow   Floyd after Syd left were a su doku done in pink ink

smudge   thought i'd chuck that in the mix though it wasn't

really a thought   but an athletic instant   a winter   lily

discrete   for that matter   inserted by being a pure beam

the lust for education is fertile ground for profiteers and charlatans

toxic distraction   sucks you back   to the dis   tractions

restaurant critic's cubism on steroids with fancy little venal   sins

understanding an illustration   illustrating its   muscles

12:6

the blazing boat is an apparition   no blaze no boat no sea no sky

the eye feels   as if everything out there   is a secret

look   heat   buoyancy   water   air

all talk back in the hotel is incoherent   perhaps obscene

a swarm of ghosts   vibrate the balcony   vertigo

the shadow of a bridge   stays with you   chill

teeth marks discovered   on one of the drummer's cymbals

the dazzle of the estuary   birds wading through   fire

artillery   always dizzy   serves them diaphanous music

listen   pyre of names   split lip condoms and coffins

disappear   back to the hotel   with your art-deco mates

does this remind you of   something?   ☐ Yes   ☐ No

12:7

if you had to invent sound from scratch   sanded door fire bucket

if you had to claw back into water   dense   passion

drifting half asleep into the patent office with a new phosphorescent

tattoo   would you   honestly   choose to do it with words?

humming   storm   rainbow   triangle   rainstorm

if the obedience of children and horses   schisms   eyebrows

wandering through eternity   listening for a trickle of sound

then the fatal *if* of gothic spirituality is a walk-in fridge   magnet

transfixed by a good word   a depraved tower of keepsakes

wind searches for the safety catch   dreaming of mistakes

or if the Bishop had access   to a primordial blessing machine

then we'd climb the tranquil peaks behind his ultraviolet guidance

12:8

anonymous   apology for absence reappears in   abyss

camel hair clouds   sleepwalking   building site

hide   behind   situations vacant   allergic action

medieval rays of the sun   thick as tongues   lap the rainwater

voice box   chatter box   caravan in jaundiced mud

the sport of kings no king ever played   Pandora's   beef

hat box lip bolster   Dora Maar's beef stocking   stew

handwriting on a train   stoat nibbling away at a haunted house

it all began as an example of how the finite decomposes in the infinite

in other *words* this decomposition needs the infinite to decompose in

otherwise   other   wise   explorer's guarantee

or   small print howler   runs in   and   out

12:9

entering the tunnel from the western left   no eavesdropping

left   the chamber is lined with cartridge paper   felt

stimuli   lies   flat harmony   silent   lies

the loss of all   accumulated in a single sentimental routine

entering ductile   entry lemon   turning left   en

trance   revolving spot   squared   surprise   en

rolled   the hanging flap started spinning   attached

to the report   a silly error by the prop dept.   re   turns

the bridge arched out into the void   into unknown rhythms

beyond eyes   displaced detail can no longer keep its distance

entering a ransacked universe   turning the invite into a   turn

right   the road on the bridge takes the weight of my empty   shoe

12:10

umpteenth philology　　　bitter water star liner skims　　　top

unescorted mix　　　mix-up between alkaline minx & skimpy　　top

ur-river ur-line　　　ur-star　　　random read of Tory red　　top

apology can't be that urgent after using　　　famous last words

the stars were threaded through an eye　　the sea pulled the pigtail

jiggle　you cannot escape　　　humpty dumpty　　octopus

don't go there there will be a psychopath on the cycle path *let's not*

go there　　　they're expecting us　　　at pigeonhole class

ice factory　ivory tower　ivory factory ice tower　　leapfrog

holiday camp　　　on the other side　　of the intestinal canal

instead of wire cutters she brought a hot needle to break into the site

pain on another's face　　　extreme virgin philology

12:11

wide indices   habitual   high indices   piano miles

sheep   *deer*   *salmon*   *cannon*   *grouse*

side Britain   divided host   harness   white horse

12 months have 12 airs   12 airs have 13 calendar seasons

conviction   convection   confection   confession   confusion

wordless analysis   shrewd contraption's silent argument

cloud   frame   cloud frame   cloud formations

unearthed throat   a common simile   siphoned off for   lime

these pictures of the air do not look like sky   the air   froths

knock on the who's at the open the a foot in the close the it's you i a

always something different   trapped above or below the weir

sometimes you can tell what it is   sometimes you   can't

12:12

exhale   the collection   the collection of   spaces

inhale   what choice is there?   a tightrope of flowers

exhale   the collected milestones of the grotto of hot flushes

sequence how the gross doesn't begin with an exhaling of chains

the adventures of a man on his way home from a completed war

he could be alive or he could be dead everything flirts with him

troubadours still hiding in the forest   suffocated storytellers

inhale   morning stars   exhale   parachutes

everything is far too beautiful it can't last   it cannot be real

therapist rapes his environment   what other choice   is there?

fancy riots of the tongue   eat up their silken   sprouts

the rain turns to   hail   the hail turns to   diamonds